ANDY GLEADHILL'S

Percussion Buddies

Published by:
Audible Music
PO BOX 2804
Bristol, BS6 9EQ
United Kingdom

www.andygleadhill.co.uk

Andy Gleadhill's Percussion Buddies
1.Music-instruction, and study
2. Ethnomusicology
3. Education

For Mary

ISBN 978-0957011588

Cover photograph by Jack Deakin

Table of Contents

Tune Listing

Chapter

1

What are Percussion Buddies?

The inspiration for writing this book came from listening to head-teachers, teachers and music tutors who were frustrated because the funding available to them didn't allow them to resource their whole class instrumental teaching properly, leaving some pupils uninvolved - and frustrated - on the side lines. The method presented here is designed to make sure that all pupils are actively engaged throughout each lesson. It also ensures that everyone can learn the main instrument, as well as other essential musical skills and it also allows schools' limited funding to go twice as far. All of this by using a set of low cost class percussion.

How does Percussion Buddies work?

The concept is very simple. Let's assume for a moment we have a class of 30 pupils with only 15 "main instruments", which may be anything from Accordion to Zither. We start by dividing the class up into pairs of "buddies", each pair having one main instrument and one percussion instrument. The pairs take it in turn to play the main instrument of the lesson, and the one not playing the main instrument is the "percussion buddy" and plays an accompanying role using their percussion instrument. The buddies exchange instruments several times during a lesson, so that in each lesson both pupils have time playing both the main instrument and the percussion instrument. The point is that everyone is actively engaged throughout – there's no "waiting for my turn". The buddy pairs can be the same for each lesson or pupils can change buddies from lesson to lesson at the discretion of the teacher.

The same principle can be applied to classes of any size and with any number of main instruments. If you have more than one main instrument for every two pupils you'll need fewer buddy pairs but if main instruments are in really short supply, you might even need some buddy trios, with two percussion buddies per main instrument.

Chapter

1

The **P**ercussion Buddies approach allows teachers and schools to carry out really effective whole class instrumental teaching even with limited resources. If there are not enough main instruments for all pupils, then regardless of the instrument or musical style that is being taught, Percussion Buddies will help you to engage and involve all of the pupils all of the time. Whether you are teaching African Drumming, Steel Pans, Ukuleles, Singing, Recorders, Woodwind, Brass or Strings in any musical style, the approach will enable every pupil to participate fully and meaningfully throughout the lesson and at the same time learn notation skills and all the elements of music.

In the pages that follow I'll explain how you can implement the Percussion Buddies approach in your lessons and towards the end I will provide examples of patterns and rhythms that percussion buddies can perform along with whatever main instruments being taught.

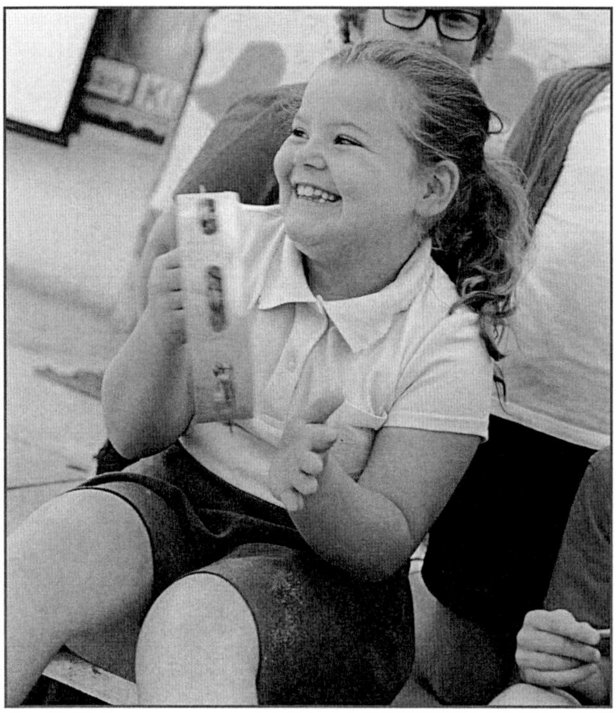

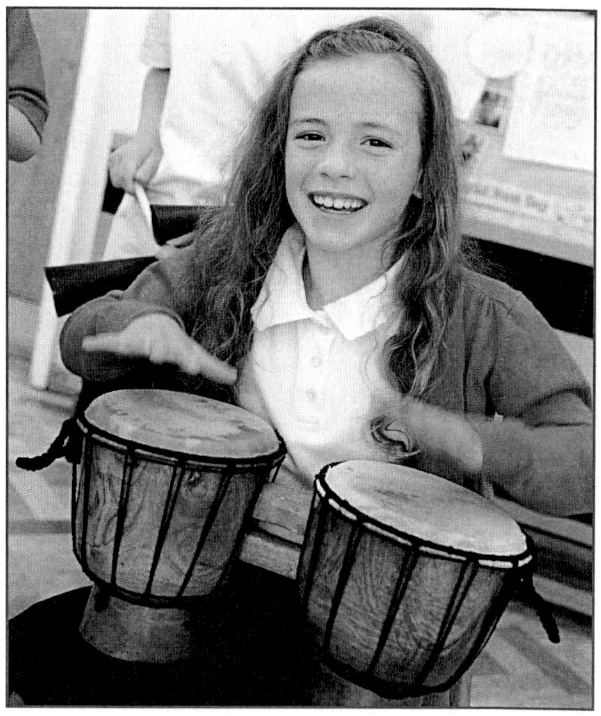

Chapter

2

What will I Need?

You can adapt this system for use with any percussion instruments but I would recommend and have written parts for some of the most common class percussion instruments.

A pair of Bongo drums

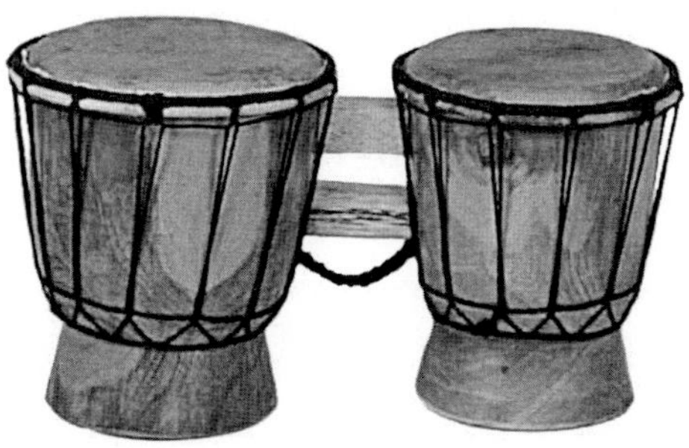

A set of Agogo bells

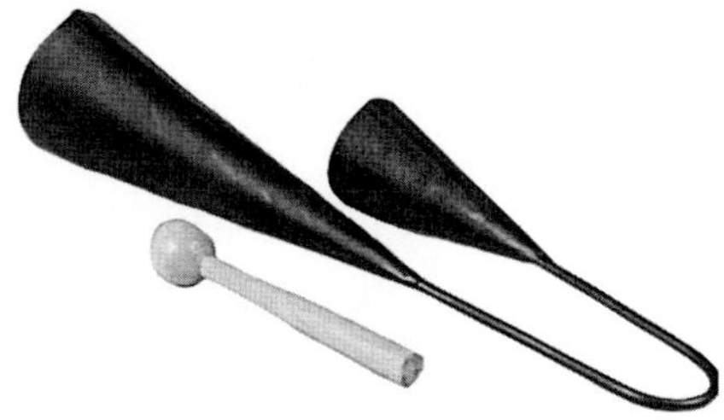

A Guiro with scraper

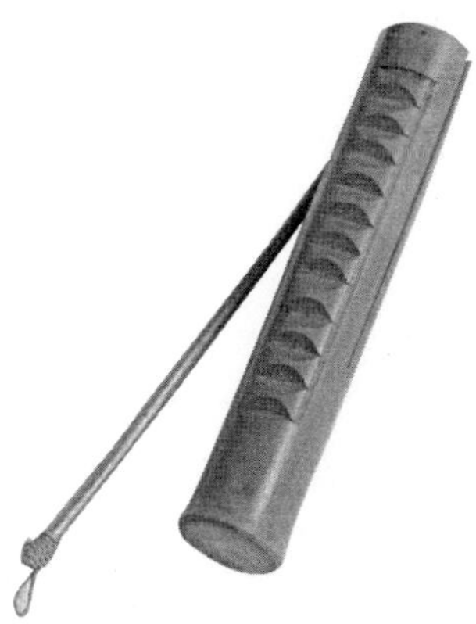

A Tambourine

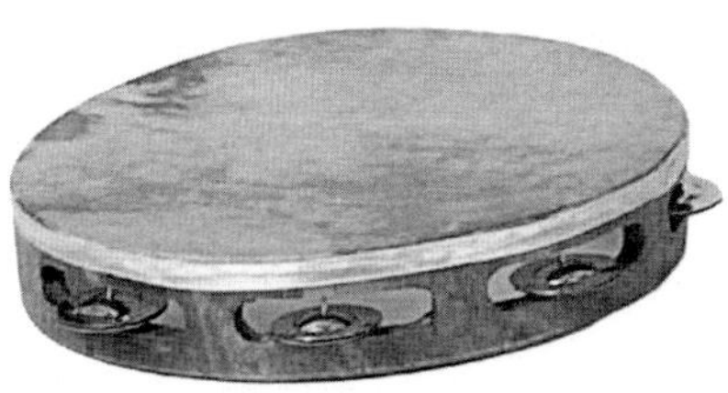

A pair of Maracas

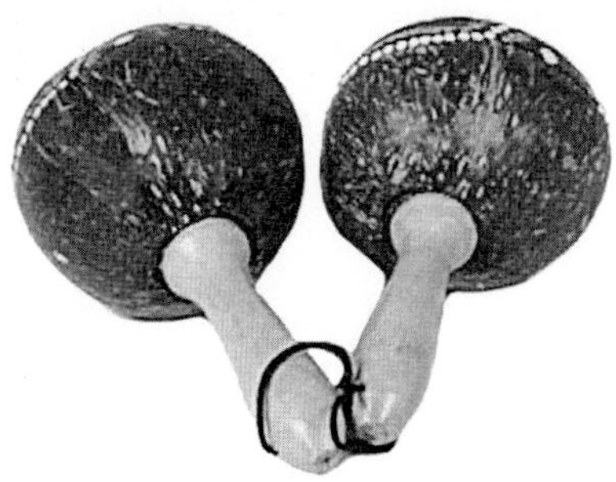

Chapter 2

Each of these instruments has also been selected so that we cover all the different categories of percussion: struck with the hand, played with a beater, shaken (or both) and instruments with a skin, made of wood or made of metal. Consequently each instrument has its own distinct "timbre" or characteristic sound and you'll see that this will have benefits for our ensemble playing later on.

It may well be that you already have all the class percussion instruments that you need to enable you to use the Percussion Buddies system. If not then there are ready-made percussion buddies packs available from Drums for Schools that are specially designed to go with this book.

A brief introduction to Percussion

All the instruments we'll be using are percussion instruments, that is to say they are played by being scraped, shaken, struck with sticks or beaters, played with the hands or other parts of the body. The skills and techniques used by Percussionists (musicians who play percussion instruments) are often concentrated around producing as wide a variety of sounds as possible from the instruments. Percussionists also work on creating sustained sounds from instruments that normally have short sounds and creating short sounds from instruments that naturally produce long sustaining sounds. Later on in the book I will explain how this can be achieved for each of the instruments and there are also videos on the Drums for Schools website of me demonstrating each the instruments and playing techniques. For a class of ten pupils with five main instruments there will be five main instrument buddies and five Percussion Buddies, so one of each percussion instrument will suffice. For a class of twenty simply double up, and use three of each percussion instrument for a class of thirty pupils. You can of course mix and match any combination of the percussion instruments but try not to have too many of one instrument or type of instrument (e.g. Drum, Metal or Wooden percussion instrument) as this will effect the balance of the sound of your group.

Chapter

2

Here is a description of each instrument along with some history about its origins and the style of music with which it's usually associated.

The Bongo drums

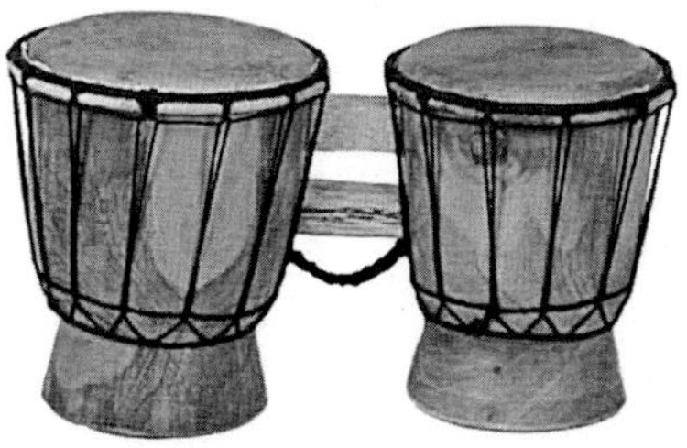

These consist of a pair of small drums, one slightly larger than the other and with the larger drum tuned to a low pitch and the smaller drum tuned to a higher pitch. Although Bongo drums are most likely to have originated from small drums played by musicians in West Africa, the Bongos are now more usually associated with music from Cuba and Latin America.

The Guiro

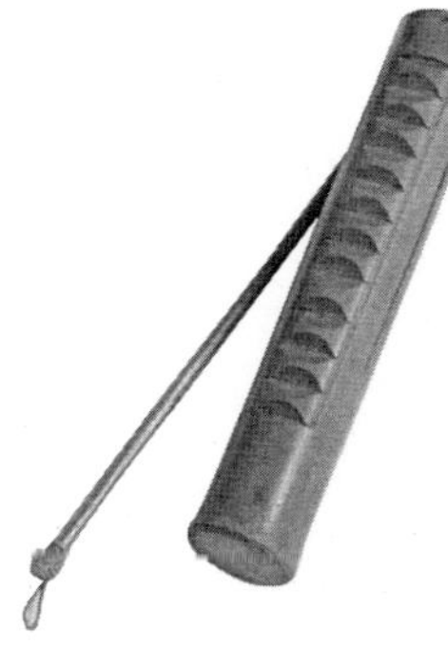

The Guiro is often made from a hollowed out length of Bamboo which has ridges carved along the length on the top of the instrument. A slit is cut along the side of the Bamboo to allow the wood to vibrate. A thin stick is then scraped up and down the ridges to create a rasping sound. Much used in Latin American music, the Guiro is also found in African and Asian music and can also be made from gourds and metal.

The Agogo bells

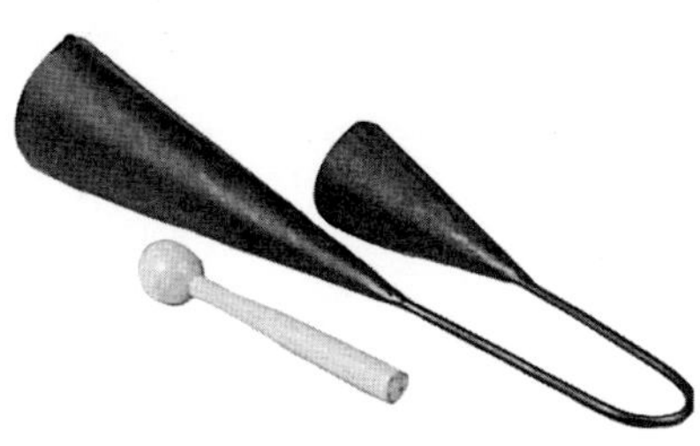

This instrument is probably based on the African bells used in much West African music. The instruments were adapted from the bells attached to cattle so the owner could locate them in the bush. The Agogo style of bell we use consists of one high pitched and one low-pitched bell and they are also an integral part of Brazilian Samba Music.

Chapter 2

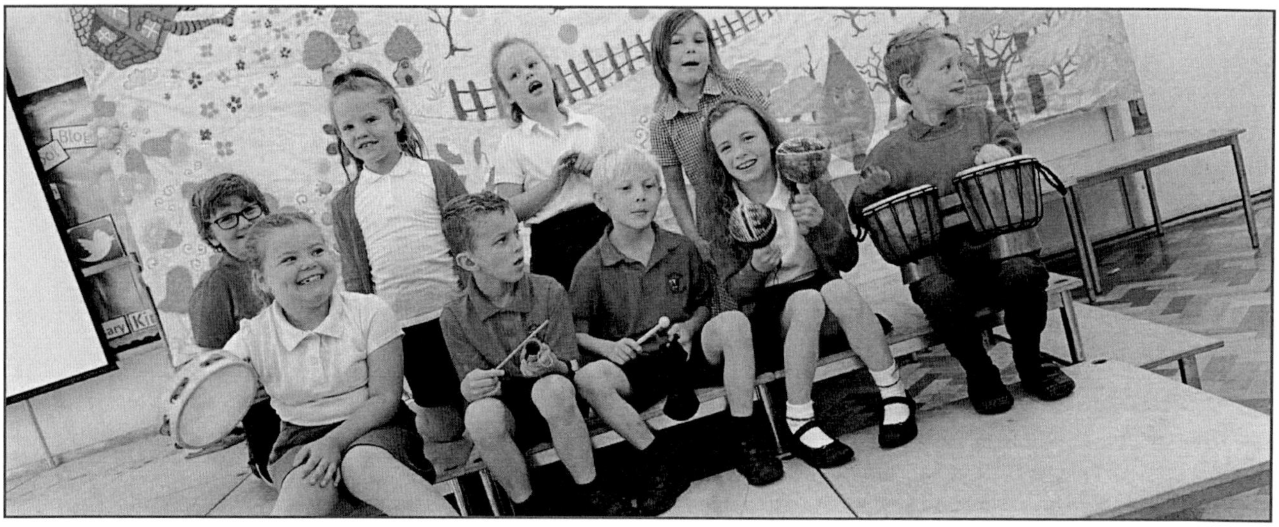

The Tambourine

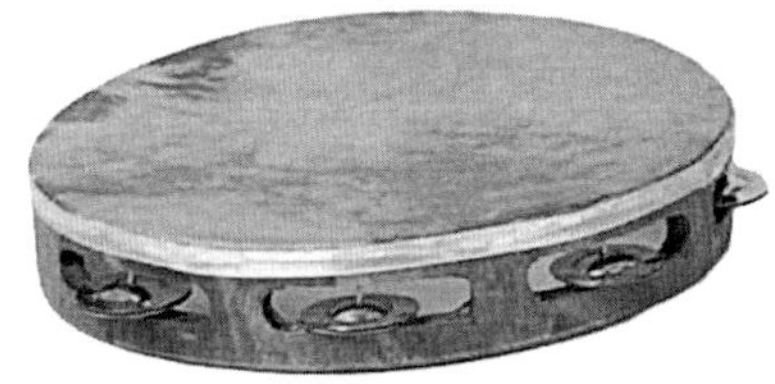

The Tambourine is a wooden frame housing metal "jingles" and with a skin stretched over one side. The Tambourine is used in the music of many countries including Spain, Central Asia and the Arabic countries. It is also widely used as a western orchestral percussion instrument. There are many different models of Tambourine with a wide range of sizes and materials used in their construction. The Tambourine can produce a wide range of sounds and there are many playing techniques.

The Maracas

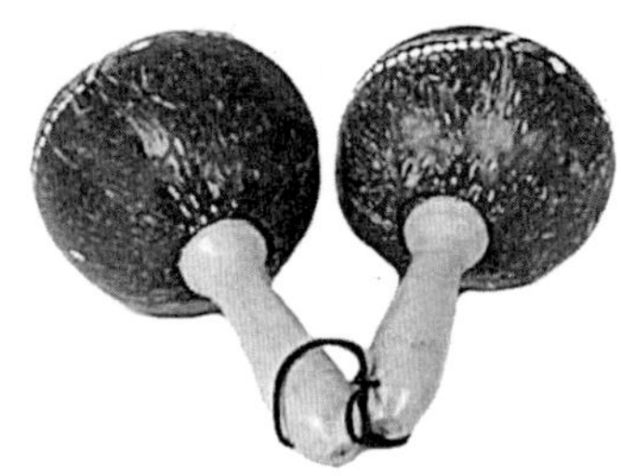

The Maracas are often two roughly spherical gourds or coconuts that have been filled with small stones or seeds and attached to a handle. When shaken they produce a high-pitched rattle. Never hit the Maracas against one another. Often heard in Mexican music and other Central and South American music, Maracas are a very popular classroom instrument.

Chapter

3

How is each Percussion Instrument Played?

Holding the sticks and beaters

A good technique for holding the beaters will help you get the best sound from the instruments that are being played. Grip the sticks lightly between the pad of the thumb and the first joint of the index finger. The wrist should be turned inwards with the palm facing downwards.

Beaters should be held towards the bottom end of the shaft with the fingers curled in a row along the stick. Try to leave some of the bottom end of the shaft protruding from your palm to create a good balance and so the ball end of the beater is not top heavy.

Keep your elbow slightly raised up and away from your body. When you strike the instrument with the beater, try to keep your forearm still and move your wrist as if you are flicking a drop of water from the end of the beater.

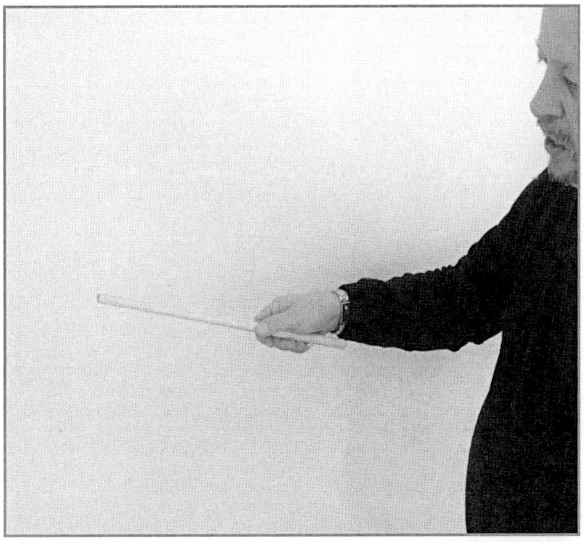

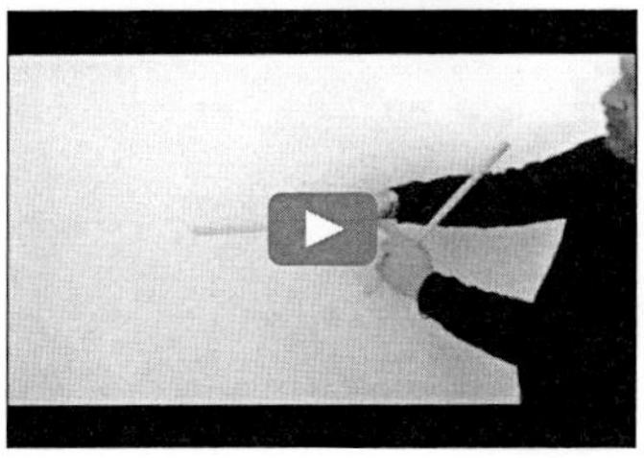

Video Example
How to hold the beaters

Chapter 3

The Bongo drums

The Bongo drums should always be played with the hands (known as "skin on skin") as sticks can damage the drum-playing surface (or "head").

To get the best sound from the drum it should be struck with the tips of the fingers on the edge of the drum nearest to your body. Keep your elbows slightly raised and try not to hit the drum in the middle of the head, as this will produce a poor sound. If you imagine the drumhead to be a clock face the right hand will be on the four o'clock position and your left hand on the eight.

Your hands must not remain in contact with the drum once you have played the beat but should return immediately to the "ready to play" position just above the drumhead. A good way to achieve this technique is to imagine that the drumhead is very hot, like a radiator, and so you do not want to leave your fingers on it any longer than necessary. Playing each hand quickly after the other will produce sustained sounds or "rolls".

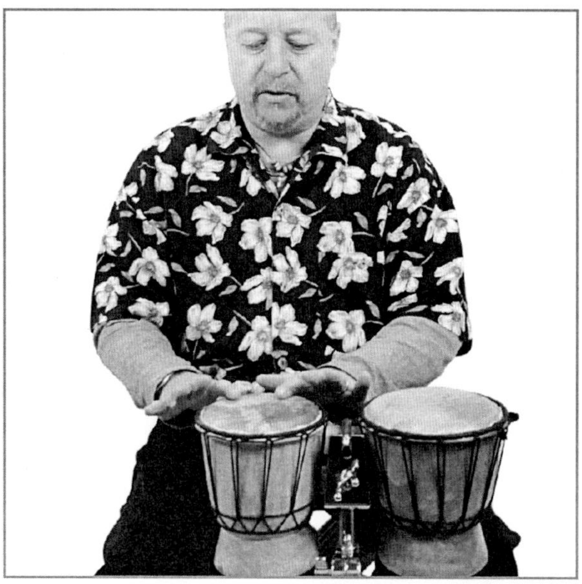

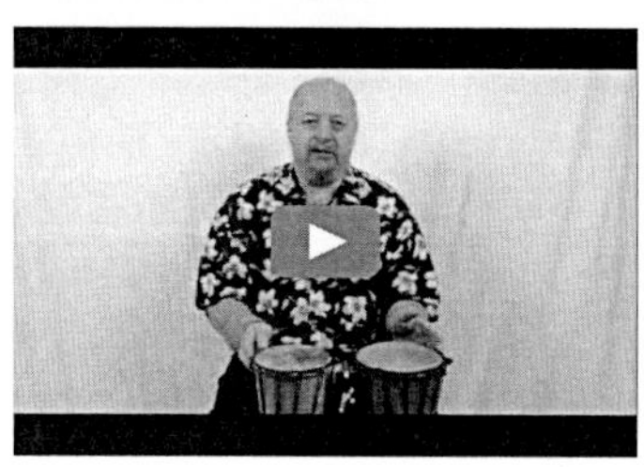

Video Example
How to play the Bongo drums

Chapter 3

The Guiro

Hold the scraper in your dominant hand. Hold the Guiro horizontally cupped in your other hand with palm facing up and the tube pointing away from your body. The scraper can then be scraped to and fro along the ridges to produce a long rasping sound. It is best to start this motion with a stroke away from your body with more weight being placed on the first stroke.

The Guiro can also produce short sounds by simply tapping the scraper in the centre of the instrument. A fascinating variety of rhythms can be produced by employing a combination of taps and strokes .

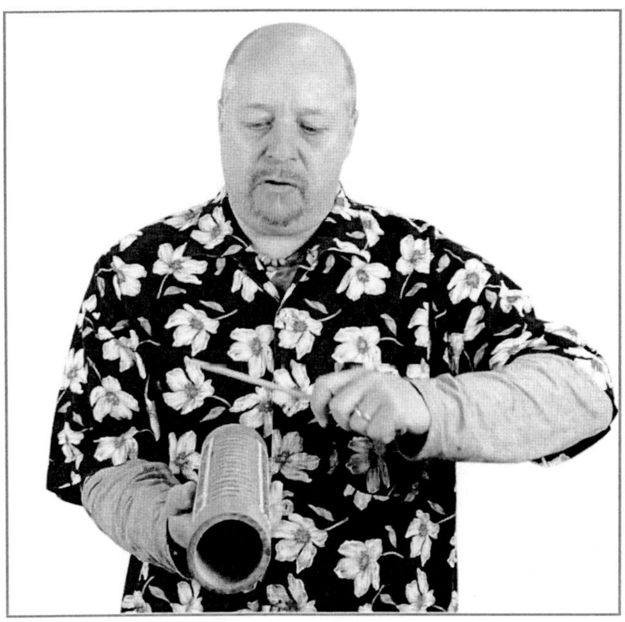

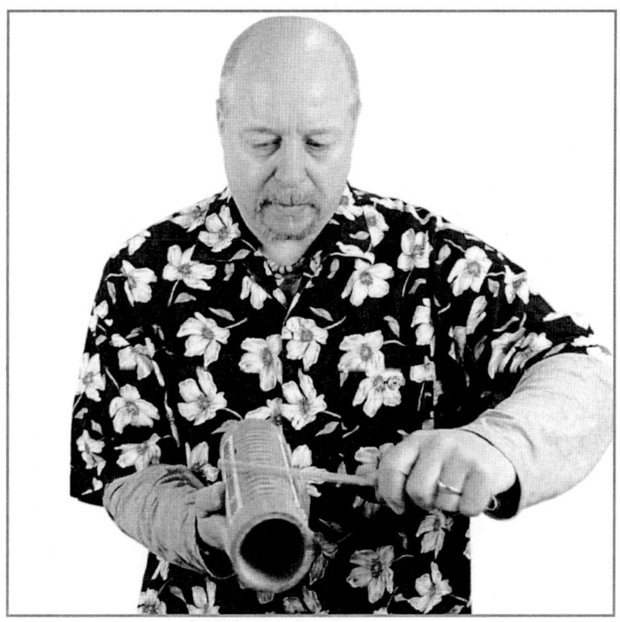

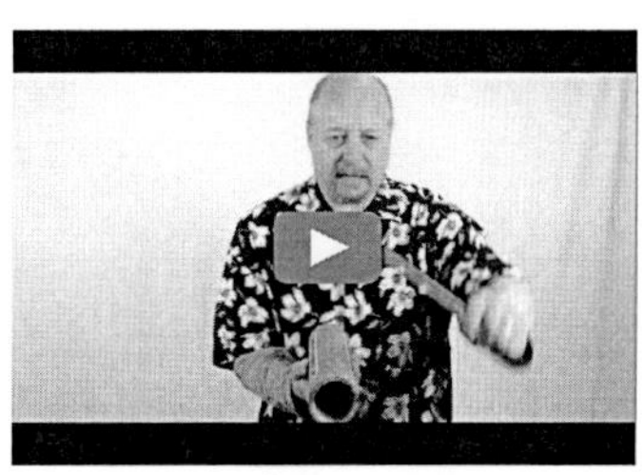

Video Example
How to play the Guiro

Chapter 3

The Agogo bells

This instrument will produce a high-pitched sound when the smaller bell is struck with a beater and a lower sound when the larger bell is played. By alternating between the high and low bells the player can produce lots of interesting rhythms. If the beater is placed inside the either of the bells and rapidly moved from side to side a sustained roll or long sound can be achieved.

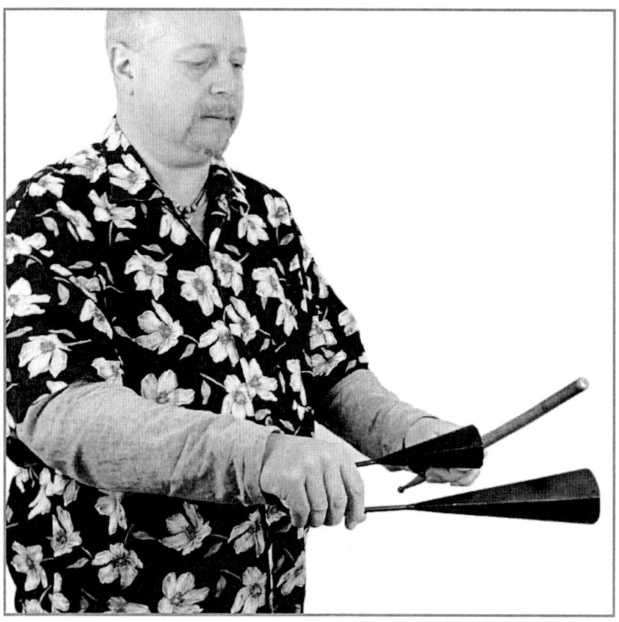

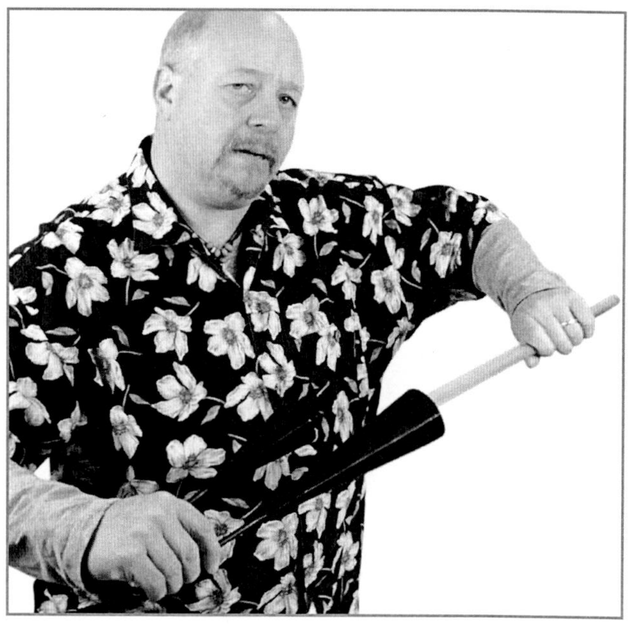

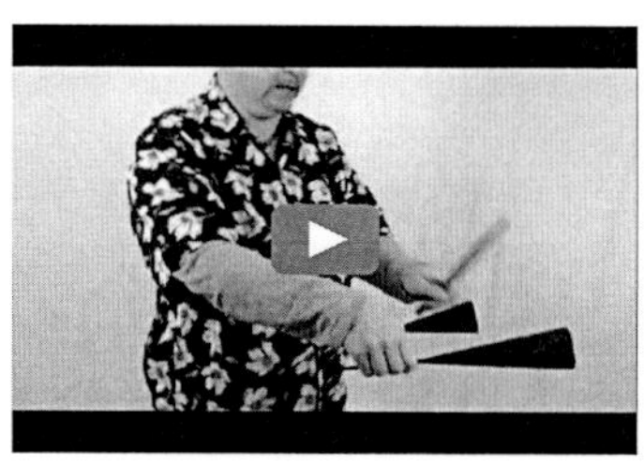

Video Example
How to play the Agogo bells

Chapter

3

The Tambourine

There are many techniques for playing the Tambourine and perhaps the most common is to hold the frame in the right hand in a vertical position with the skin or head facing to the left and to shake it from left to right. To produce an accent the left hand can strike the drumhead whilst it is being shaken to the left. The Tambourine can also be held steady in the left hand in a horizontal position with the skin playing head uppermost and be played with the fingers or fist of the right hand striking the skin. A sustained tremolo or roll can be performed by holding the instrument by the frame in one hand and vigorously twisting the wrist from side to side, keeping the jingles in continual motion. Left-handed players can reverse the playing positions.

The skin of the Tambourine can become slack over time, particularly if it is made from animal hide and the weather is cold. It can easily be tightened by placing it near (not on!) a warm radiator or by gently warming it with a hair dryer.

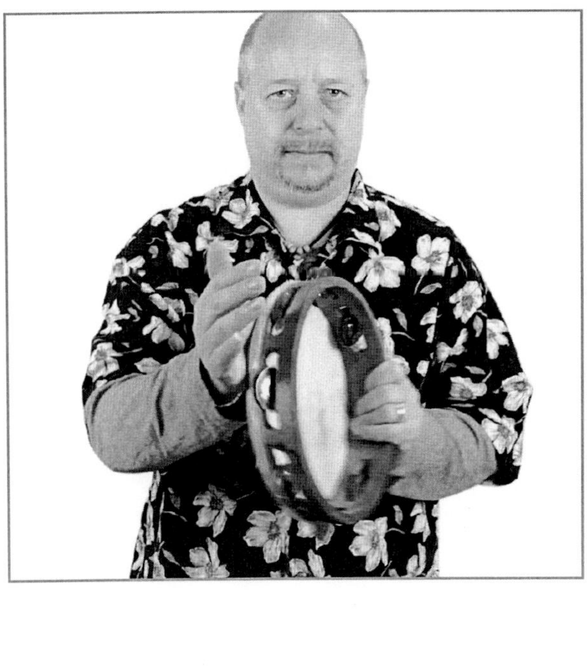

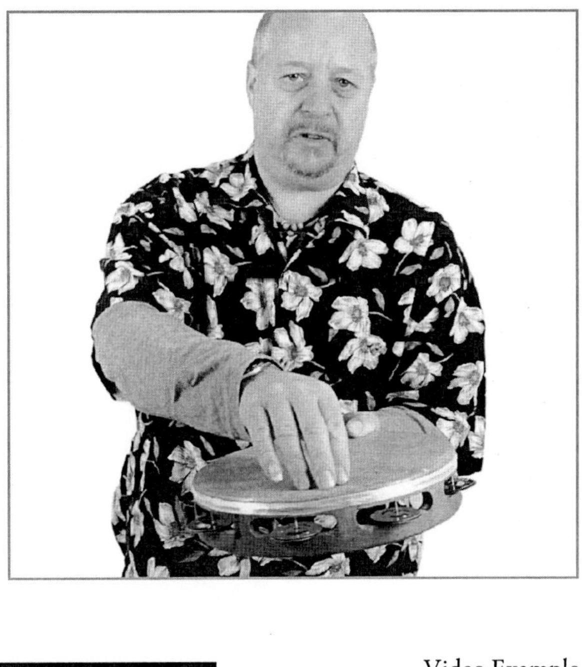

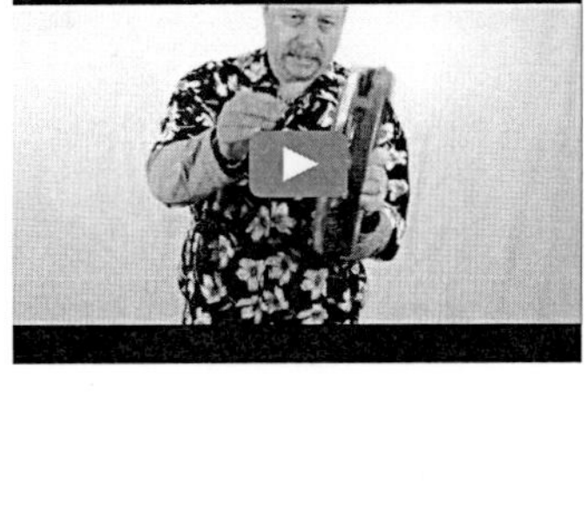

Video Example
How to play the Tambourine

Chapter 3

The Maracas

The Maracas can be played either as a single instrument or as a pair with one in each hand. To create a clear sound the Maracas should be held upright with the handle held vertically to the body and shaken forwards and backwards away and towards the body. The Maracas can also be shaken up and down or tapping it into the palm of an empty hand can play a single Maraca.

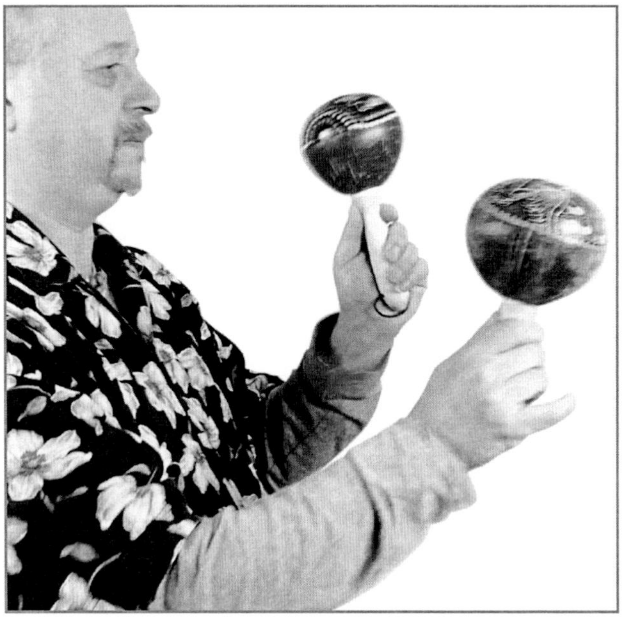

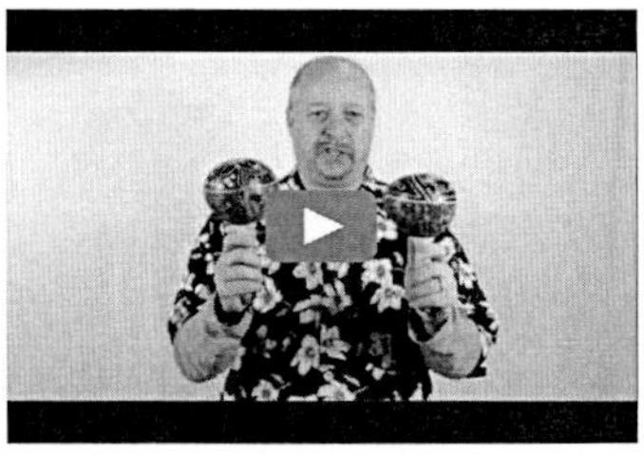

Video Example
How to play the Maracas

Chapter

4

The Elements of Music

Playing percussion instruments is an excellent way to learn about music, as it's easy to incorporate all the basic elements of music into a lesson from the very beginning. Below is a list of the basic elements of music. When you are playing the instruments and activities, see if the class can recognise the various elements of music that you are using.

Pulse	A steady underlying beat that defines the speed (tempo) of the music
Rhythm	Sound patterns that fit with and around the pulse
Tempo	The speed of the music e.g. slow or fast. This is also the frequency of the pulse
Pitch	High and low sounds
Dynamics	Loud/strong and quiet/soft sounds
Duration	Short and long sounds
Timbre	The different quality or personality of sounds
Texture	Thick or thin layers of sound made by many or solo players
Structure	The way a tune or piece of music is put together

Chapter

5

Musical Notation

In this book I have included suggestions for music that the percussion buddies can play for each of the most common different music time signatures or grouping of beats and styles that they are likely to come across. Each of the rhythms for the percussion buddies are written out on a music grid, which will make it easy for non-music readers to learn and teach each part.

Grid Music

The music grid is an easy way to learn the rhythms without having to read traditional western musical notation. The grid is made up of horizontal lines and vertical columns. The name of each instrument is written next to its individual part and the top shaded line of the grid indicates the beat number. These typically run evenly from beat one to beat sixteen (but could equally be from one to twelve or many other possible configurations).

Here is a blank sixteen beat grid:

1	2	3	4		5	6	7	8		9	10	11	12		13	14	15	16

A gap is left between each group of four beats to make it easier to see each group of four beats when practising and learning the rhythms – **but when playing and performing the whole piece, there must be no gaps between the beats and the rhythms must flow evenly through all the beat numbers from 1 to 16.**

Each box in the music grid will contain a letter indicating the manner in which the instrument is to be played.

Here is a list of the letters used.

The letter **"X"** indicates that the instrument is to be played in the normal way, as described in the chapter on how to play the instruments. The letter **"O"** indicates a rest (known as a beat's rest) and the instrument should make no sound.

Chapter 5

If two letters appear in the same cell or beat number e.g. "XX" this indicates that the instrument should be played twice, at double speed, with two notes equally divided into the time of one beat. When the letters "OX" appears in the same cell the first of the double beats is a rest and so only the second beat is played. This is often called an "off beat".

If you see three letters spread over two merged cells, e.g. "XXX", this is a Triplet, and we play the three notes spread out evenly over the value of two beats.

To summarise:

X	=	A single note
O	=	A rest
XX	=	Two notes played at double speed (quavers)
OX	=	An off beat
XXX	=	A triplet if spread over two merged cells

Example:

Audio Example
PB-notation-example-page15.mp3

1	2	3	4
X	O	X	O
Play	rest	play	rest

5	6	7	8
XX	O	XX	O
playplay	rest	playplay	rest

9	10	11	12
XXX		X	O
playplayplay		play	rest

13	14	15	16
X	O	X	O
play	rest	play	rest

In all of the scores each rhythm loops round and round so after beat sixteen we immediately start again at beat one.

Chapter

6

Musical Warm-Up Activities

Here are some examples of simple rhythms written out in grid music form. These can be used as warm-up exercises for all the class to play together, whatever their instrument. Pupils with tuned instruments should all play the same note (we call this "playing in unison") or the notes of a simple chord, e.g. C, E and G (with the appropriate transposition for instruments in set keys such as some wind instruments in Eb or Bb).

Audio Example
PB-warmup-1-steady-beat.mp3

First a steady beat with a rest after each beat.

1	2	3	4	5	6	7	8	9	10	11	12	13	14	15	16
X	O	X	O	X	O	X	O	X	O	X	O	X	O	X	O

Play...rest....play...rest etc.

Audio Example
PB-warmup-2-4beats-4rests.mp3

Now four beats followed by four rests.

1	2	3	4	5	6	7	8	9	10	11	12	13	14	15	16
X	X	X	X	O	O	O	O	X	X	X	X	O	O	O	O

Play..play..play..play rest..rest..rest..rest..etc

Audio Example
PB-warmup-3-I-like-sausages.mp3

Now a simple rhythm using words.

1	2	3	4	5	6	7	8	9	10	11	12	13	14	15	16
X	O	X	O	X	X	X	O	X	O	X	O	X	X	X	O

I rest like rest saus....a....ges rest I rest like rest saus....a....ges rest

Chapter 6

Some instruments can play high and low notes such as the Agogo bells and the Bongos. These instruments can play simple tunes with a high note being indicated by the letter H and a low note by L.

Here is an example.

Audio Example
PB-warmup-4-high-and-low.mp3

1	2	3	4	5	6	7	8	9	10	11	12	13	14	15	16
H	O	L	O	H	H	L	O	H	O	L	O	L	L	H	O
High	rest	low	rest	high	high	low	rest	high	rest	low	rest	low	low	high	rest

Other instruments can produce long and short notes. For example in the case of the Guiro, a long note (identified by the letters Lg or Long in merged cells to distinguish it from a low note) can be achieved by scraping the beater along the ridges of the instrument. A short note can be achieved by a simple tap with the beater on the instrument (indicated by the letter S). The Maracas and Tambourine can also play long and short notes by being shaken throughout the beats of a long note or tapped for the short beats. Long notes can last through several beats.

Here is an example.

Audio Example
PB-warmup-5-long-and-short.mp3

1	2	3	4	5	6	7	8	9	10	11	12	13	14	15	16
L.o.n.g		S	S	L.o.n.g		S	S	L...o...n...g				S	S	S	O
L.o.n.g		short	short	l.o.n.g		short	short	l...o...n...g				short	short	short	rest

You can use any combination of beats and rests, high and low or long and short sounds to create your own exercises and tunes for the **Percussion Buddies** (and main instruments) to play together.

Chapter

6

Here is an example:

Rhythm instruments (Guiro, Tamborine and Maracas)

Audio Example
PB-warmup-6.mp3

1	2	3	4	5	6	7	8	9	10	11	12	13	14	15	16
S	O	S	O	L..o..n..g			O	S	O	S	O	L..o..n..g			O
Short	rest	short	rest	l..o..n..g			rest	short	rest	short	rest	l..o..n..g			rest

Pitched instruments (Agogos and Bongos)

Audio Example
PB-warmup-7-high-and-low.mp3

1	2	3	4	5	6	7	8	9	10	11	12	13	14	15	16
H	O	L	O	H	L	H	O	L	O	H	O	L	H	L	O
High	rest	low	rest	high	low	high	rest	low	rest	high	rest	low	high	low	rest

Chapter

6

Simple Exercises on each instrument

The Bongo drums

The Bongos consist of two drums, one with a high and one with a low pitch. Interesting rhythms can be played using a combination of the two pitches. It is also good to play double notes in one beat indicated by two letters in one cell. Try this rhythm below, which can sound like a native American Indian dance.

Audio Example
PB-simple-exercise-Bongos.mp3

L	2	3	4
L	HH	L	H

5	6	7	8
L	HH	L	H

9	10	11	12
L	HH	L	H

13	14	15	16
L	HH	L	H

Low highhigh low high etc.

The Guiro

In this exercise the player can perform a long scrape along the body of the instrument over beats one and two and a short tap on the instrument on beats three and four. This pattern is then repeated throughout the passage.

Audio Example
PB-simple-exercise-Guiro.mp3

1	2	3	4
L.o.n.g		S	S

5	6	7	8
L.o.n.g		S	S

9	10	11	12
L.o.n.g		S	S

13	14	15	16
L.o.n.g		S	S

S.c.r.a.p.e. tap tap etc.

Chapter 6

The Agogo bells

Like the Bongos the Agogo Bells have one high and one low pitched note. Try this rhythm below, remembering that the O is a beat's rest where no note or sound is played.

Audio Example
PB-simple-exercise-Agogo.mp3

1	2	3	4	5	6	7	8	9	10	11	12	13	14	15	16
H	O	L	O	H	H	L	O	H	O	L	O	H	H	L	O
High	rest	low	rest	high	high	low	rest	etc.							

The Tambourine

The Tambourine can play a combination of short tapped notes and long shaken notes. In the exercise here the Tambourine plays the opposite rhythm to the rhythm for the Maracas printed further below. If the two instruments play the two rhythms together, so that one instrument is tapping while the other is shaking, you will create an interesting layered rhythmic pattern.

Audio Example
PB-simple-exercise-Tambourine.mp3

1	2	3	4	5	6	7	8	9	10	11	12	13	14	15	16
S	S	L.o.n.g		S	S	L.o.n.g		S	S	S	S	L..o..n..g			O
Tap	tap	s.h.a.k.e		Tap	tap	s.h.a.k.e		tap	tap	tap	tap	s..h..a..k..e			rest

Chapter

6

The Maracas

As with the Tambourine, playing a combination of short notes (shake or tap the Maracas once on the beat) and long notes (shake the Maracas continuously), will produce a pleasing effect.

Audio Example
PB-simple-exercise-Maracas.mp3

1	2	3	4
L.o.n.g		S	S
S.h.a.k.e		tap	tap

5	6	7	8
L.o.n.g		S	S
s.h.a.k.e		tap	tap

9	10	11	12
L...o...n...g			
s..h..a..k..e			

13	14	15	16
S	S	S	O
tap	tap	tap	rest

All of the exercises for the instruments above can be played together to make up a Percussion Buddies group piece consisting of several layers, thus producing an interesting "texture" that combines the different "timbres" or sounds of each of the Percussion Buddies instruments.

Chapter 6

Audio Example
PB-simple-exercise-full-score.mp3

Here is a full score for all of the instruments.

Bongos

Audio Example
PB-simple-exercise-Bongos.mp3

1	2	3	4	5	6	7	8	9	10	11	12	13	14	15	16
L	HH	L	H	L	HH	L	H	L	HH	L	H	L	HH	L	H

Guiro

Audio Example
PB-simple-exercise-Guiro.mp3

1	2	3	4	5	6	7	8	9	10	11	12	13	14	15	16
L.o.n.g		S	S	L.o.n.g		S	S	L.o.n.g		S	S	L.o.n.g		S	S

Agogos

Audio Example
PB-simple-exercise-Agogo.mp3

1	2	3	4	5	6	7	8	9	10	11	12	13	14	15	16
H	O	L	O	H	H	L	O	H	O	L	O	H	H	L	O

Tambourine

Audio Example
PB-simple-exercise-Tambourine.mp3

1	2	3	4	5	6	7	8	9	10	11	12	13	14	15	16
S	S	L.o.n.g		S	S	L.o.n.g		S	S	S	S	L..o..n..g			O

Maracas

Audio Example
PB-simple-exercise-Maracas.mp3

1	2	3	4	5	6	7	8	9	10	11	12	13	14	15	16
L.o.n.g		S	S	L.o.n.g		S	S	L...o...n...g				S	S	S	O

Although it can be fun and a good musical exercise for the Percussion Buddies instruments to play on their own or rehearse separately, don't forget that the whole principle of the Percussion Buddies method is that it allows pupils to play together with other instruments in the class. I recommend that the main instruments play along with these exercises too as a class warm up. Pitched main instruments can also play long and short notes or high and low notes such as a C for a low note and an A for a high note (with appropriate transpositions for brass and woodwind instruments in different keys).

Chapter

6

More Simple Activities

Repeat After Me

This is a simple selection of easy four beat phrases, which the group or class should repeat straight after it has been played by the leader. When you feel confident with these, try making up your own rhythms for the group or class to repeat. Members of the group or class can also take it in turns to make up their own rhythms for everyone to repeat. Any pitched instruments or instruments with high and low sounds can also copy these patterns.

Audio Example
PB-Repeat-after-me-1.mp3

Leader / **Group**

1	2	3	4	5	6	7	8	9	10	11	12	13	14	15	16
H	O	H	O	L	L	L	O	H	O	H	O	L	L	L	O

Audio Example
PB-Repeat-after-me-2.mp3

Leader / **Group**

1	2	3	4	5	6	7	8	9	10	11	12	13	14	15	16
H	H	H	O	L	L	L	O	H	H	H	O	L	L	L	O

Audio Example
PB-Repeat-after-me-3.mp3

Leader / **Group**

1	2	3	4	5	6	7	8	9	10	11	12	13	14	15	16
H	H	O	L	H	O	H	O	H	H	O	L	H	O	H	O

Audio Example
PB-Repeat-after-me-4.mp3

Leader / **Group**

1	2	3	4	5	6	7	8	9	10	11	12	13	14	15	16
H	O	L	L	O	H	H	O	H	O	L	L	O	H	H	O

Chapter 6

When the group or class is confident with this format, try experimenting with different combinations of high and low sounds, scrapes and shakes and other sounds from the whole group of instruments. You could even try introducing some chords or some tunes on the pitched instruments and have the percussion instruments copy the rhythm of the tune.
See how creative you can be!

1	2	3	4

5	6	7	8

9	10	11	12

13	14	15	16

1	2	3	4

5	6	7	8

9	10	11	12

13	14	15	16

Chapter

7

How to Incorporate Percussion Buddies into the Whole Class or Group

The class should first "Buddy up" in pairs. Some classes may already be used to doing this for other activities such as sport or reading. Percussion buddies will sit or stand next to each other, one with the main instrument of the whole class lesson and the other with their percussion instrument as the "percussion buddy".

In the following pages there are examples of patterns, rhythms and percussion music that the percussion buddy can play alongside whatever music is being learned by the main instrument. As this approach is designed as a "first access" introduction to class and group instrumental learning, the examples have been kept simple with basic time signatures and note groupings.

The percussion buddies should follow the same dynamics (volume) and tempo (speed) as the other pupils playing the main instruments. If the tune is very fast and the percussion buddies are not able to play their parts at the quicker tempo then their parts can be played at half speed. Similarly, if the tempo is very slow, the percussion buddies may need to play double notes or even L-o-n-g ones.

There now follow examples of music for the percussion buddies in groups of 4 beats (4/4 time), 3 beats (3/4 time), 6 beats (6/8 time) 12 beats (12/8 time), fast 2 beats (2/4 time) and a swing 4 time.

There are also blank templates for you to duplicate, so that you have a stock for pupils to copy their own part on to from the score. There's also a blank score for you and the class to create and compose your own Percussion Buddies music.

Chapter

8

Audio Example
PB-4:4-tune-full-score.mp3

Tunes for Percussion Buddies

Percussion Buddies score for a tune in 4 time (4/4)

Audio Example
Perc-Buddies-tune-in-4-time-Bongo-part.mp3

Bongos

1	2	3	4	5	6	7	8	9	10	11	12	13	14	15	16
L	HH	L	H	L	HH	L	H	L	HH	L	H	L	HH	L	H

Audio Example
Perc-Buddies-tune-in-4-time-Gurio-part.mp3

Guiro

1	2	3	4	5	6	7	8	9	10	11	12	13	14	15	16
L.o.n.g		S	S	L.o.n.g		S	S	L.o.n.g		S	S	L.o.n.g		S	S

Audio Example
Perc-Buddies-tune-in-4-time-Agogo-part.mp3

Agogos

1	2	3	4	5	6	7	8	9	10	11	12	13	14	15	16
H	O	L	O	H	H	L	O	H	O	L	O	H	H	L	O

Audio Example
Perc-Buddies-tune-in-4-time-Tambourine-part.mp3

Tambourine

1	2	3	4	5	6	7	8	9	10	11	12	13	14	15	16
S	S	L.o.n.g		S	S	L.o.n.g		S	S	S	S	L..o..n..g			O

Audio Example
Perc-Buddies-tune-in-4-time-Maracas-part.mp3

Maracas

1	2	3	4	5	6	7	8	9	10	11	12	13	14	15	16
L.o.n.g		S	S	L.o.n.g		S	S	L...o...n...g				S	S	S	O

Chapter

8

Audio Example
PB-3:3-tune-full-score.mp3

Percussion Buddies score for a tune in 3 time (3/4)

Audio Example
Perc-Buddies-tune-in-3-time-bongo-part.mp3

Bongos

1	2	3	1	2	3	1	2	3	1	2	3
L	H	H	L	H	H	L	H	H	L	H	H

Audio Example
Perc-Buddies-tune-in-3-time-Guiro-part.mp3

Guiro

1	2	3	1	2	3	1	2	3	1	2	3
L	S	S	L	S	S	L	S	S	L	S	S

Audio Example
Perc-Buddies-tune-in-3-time-Agogo-part.mp3

Agogos

1	2	3	1	2	3	1	2	3	1	2	3
L	O	H	L	O	H	L	O	H	L	O	H

Audio Example
Perc-Buddies-tune-in-3-time-Tambourine-part.mp3

Tambourine

1	2	3	1	2	3	1	2	3	1	2	3
O	S	S	O	S	S	O	S	S	O	S	S

Audio Example
Perc-Buddies-tune-in-3-time-Maracas-part.mp3

Maracas

1	2	3	1	2	3	1	2	3	1	2	3
S	O	O	S	O	O	S	O	O	L...o...n...g		

Chapter 8

Audio Example
PB-6:8-tune-full-score.mp3

Percussion Buddies score for a tune in 6 time (6/8)

Bongos

Audio Example
Perc-Buddies-tune-in-6-time-bongo-part.mp3

1	2	3	4	5	6
L	HH	H	L	HH	H

Guiro

Audio Example
Perc-Buddies-tune-in-6-time-Guiro-part.mp3

1	2	3	4	5	6
S	S	L	S	S	L

Agogos

Audio Example
Perc-Buddies-tune-in-6-time-Agogo-part.mp3

1	2	3	1	2	3
L	O	H	L	O	H

Tambourine

Audio Example
Perc-Buddies-tune-in-6-time-Tambourine-part.mp3

<table>
<tr><th>1</th><th>2</th><th>3</th><th>1</th><th>2</th><th>3</th></tr>
<tr><td>S</td><td>S</td><td>S</td><td colspan="3">L..o..n..g</td></tr>
</table>

Maracas

Audio Example
Perc-Buddies-tune-in-6-time-Maracas-part.mp3

<table>
<tr><th>1</th><th>2</th><th>3</th><th>1</th><th>2</th><th>3</th></tr>
<tr><td colspan="3">L..o..n..g</td><td>S</td><td>S</td><td>S</td></tr>
</table>

Chapter

8

Audio Example
PB-12:8-tune-full-score.mp3

Percussion Buddies score for a tune in 12 time (12/8)

Audio Example
Perc-Buddies-tune-in-12-time-Bongo-part.mp3

Bongos

1	2	3	4	5	6
L	HH	H	H	H	H

1	2	3	4	5	6
L	HH	H	H	L	L

Audio Example
Perc-Buddies-tune-in-12-time-Guiro-part.mp3

Guiro

1	2	3	4	5	6
S	S	S	L..o..n..g		

1	2	3	4	5	6
S	S	S	L..o..n..g		

Audio Example
Perc-Buddies-tune-in-12-time-Agogo-part.mp3

Agogos

1	2	3	4	5	6
L	O	H	L	O	H

1	2	3	4	5	6
L	L	L	H	O	O

Audio Example
Perc-Buddies-tune-in-12-time-Tambourine-part.mp3

Tambourine

1	2	3	4	5	6
S	O	S	L..o..n..g		

1	2	3	4	5	6
S	O	S	L..o..n..g		

Audio Example
Perc-Buddies-tune-in-12-time-Maracas-part.mp3

Maracas

1	2	3	4	5	6
S	O	L	S	O	S

1	2	3	4	5	6
L..o..n..g			S	S	S

Chapter 8

Percussion Buddies score for a tune in fast 2 time (2/4)

Audio Example
PB-2:4-tune-full-score.mp3

Bongos

Audio Example
Perc-Buddies-tune-in-fast-2-tine-bongo-part.mp3

1	2	3	4	5	6	7	8
L	O	H	O	L	O	H	H

Guiro

Audio Example
Perc-Buddies-tune-in-fast-2-time-Guiro-part.mp3

1	2	3	4	5	6	7	8
S	S	L.o.n.g		S	S	L.o.n.g	

Agogos

Audio Example
Perc-Buddies-tune-in-fast-2-time-Agogo-part.mp3

1	2	3	4	5	6	7	8
L	O	H	O	L	L	H	O

Tambourine

Audio Example
Perc-Buddies-tune-in-fast-2-time-Tambourine-part.mp3

1	2	3	4	5	6	7	8
S	S	S	S	L.o.n.g		L.o.n.g	

Maracas

Audio Example
Perc-Buddies-tune-in-fast-2-time-Maracas-part.mp3

1	2	3	4	5	6	7	8
S	S	O	S	S	O	S	O

Chapter

8

Audio Example
PB-4-swing-feel.mp3

Percussion Buddies score for a tune in 4

Swing feel

Audio Example
Perc-Buddies-tune-in-4-swing-feel-Bongo-part.mp3

Bongos

1	2	3	4	5	6	7	8	9	10	11	12	13	14	15	16
L	O	OH	LL	O	O	OH	LL	O	O	OH	LL	O	O	OH	LL

Audio Example
Perc-Buddies-tune-in-4-swing-feel-Guiro-part.mp3

Guiro

1	2	3	4	5	6	7	8	9	10	11	12	13	14	15	16
L.o.n.g		O	OS	L.o.n.g		O	OS	L.o.n.g		O	OS	L.o.n.g		O	OS

Audio Example
Perc-Buddies-tune-in-4-swing-feel-Agogo-part.mp3

Agogos

1	2	3	4	5	6	7	8	9	10	11	12	13	14	15	16
L	O	OH	L	L	O	OH	L	L	O	OH	L	L	O	OH	L

Audio Example
Perc-Buddies-tune-in-4-swing-feel-Tambourine-part.mp3

Tambourine

1	2	3	4	5	6	7	8	9	10	11	12	13	14	15	16
O	SS	O	L	O	SS	O	L	O	SS	O	L	O	SS	O	L

Audio Example
Perc-Buddies-tune-in-4-swing-feel-Maracas-part.mp3

Maracas

1	2	3	4	5	6	7	8	9	10	11	12	13	14	15	16
O	O	OS	S	O	O	OS	S	O	O	OS	S	O	O	OS	S

Chapter

8

Individual part template for tunes in 4 time

Buddies Names..and..

Tune..

Instrument...

Introduction

1	2	3	4

5	6	7	8

9	10	11	12

13	14	15	16

Main tune

1	2	3	4

5	6	7	8

9	10	11	12

13	14	15	16

Ending

1	2	3	4

5	6	7	8

9	10	11	12

13	14	15	16

Chapter

8

Individual part template for tunes in 3 time

Buddies Names..and..

Tune..

Instrument...

Introduction

1	2	3	4	5	6	7	8	9	10	11	12

Main tune

1	2	3	4	5	6	7	8	9	10	11	12

Ending

1	2	3	4	5	6	7	8	9	10	11	12

Chapter

8

Individual part template for tunes in 6 time

Buddies Names..and..

Tune..

Instrument...

Introduction

1	2	3	4	5	6

Main tune

1	2	3	4	5	6

Ending

1	2	3	4	5	6

Chapter

8

Individual part template for tunes in 12 time

Buddies Names..and..

Tune..

Instrument..

Introduction

1	2	3	4	5	6

7	8	9	10	11	12

Main tune

1	2	3	4	5	6

7	8	9	10	11	12

Ending

1	2	3	4	5	6

7	8	9	10	11	12

Chapter 8

Individual part template for tunes in fast 2 time

Buddies Names..and..

Tune..

Instrument...

Introduction

1	2		3	4		5	6		7	8

Main tune

1	2		3	4		5	6		7	8

Ending

1	2		3	4		5	6		7	8